OUTSIDE THE WIRE

A U.S. Marine's Collection of
Combat Poems & Short Stories
Volume II

by
Justin T. Eggen

Untitled
Matt Hudson

For Nimish,
&
To the generation of lost souls
who found purpose through combat.

This book is for you.

Follow Me, Tread Lightly

FOREWORD
by Andrew Lutz

I can't feel my right arm. I look at my watch. It's noon. I've been sweeping this road for seven hours. "We must have covered over ten clicks by now," I mutter to myself as I transfer my metal detector to my left arm. I look up and see Edmison taking a knee, pulling out his bayonet to inspect a patch of earth where he suspects there might be an IED. I crouch to make sure that I'm ready for the ambush that could begin any moment. Wiping the sweat from my brow, I shoulder my weapon and scan the terrain. Irrigation canals and hedgerows stretch across the valley for miles. Unlimited cover and concealment for the Taliban and we're in the middle of this road, completely exposed. Edmison gets up from the dirt. No bomb. Standing up and slinging my rifle, I continue my sweep, covering my section of this dirt road that the Marine Corps had named "route cowboys." All these routes are named after football teams. Mike had been killed on route redskins. The lights go out. "Lutz! Lutz! Are you good to go?" I hear as I feel someone violently shaking me. I look up. It's Gunny Eagle. He looks relieved. I'm lying on the road, disoriented. I look at my hands and they're bloody. My first thought is of my rifle, my lifeline. It's ten feet in front of me, next to a crater. They didn't get me. Not this time.

I can say with confidence that the transition from Marine to civilian is not an easy one. In May it will be ten years since Justin and I arrived on Parris Island, South Carolina as naïve, bellicose teenagers, ready to take the fight to the Taliban. In the ten years since our induction into the Marine Corps we have both deployed to Southern Afghanistan twice as engineers, working in areas of operation ranging from Garmsir, Marjah, Musa Qala and Sangin. During the time of our tours, from 2009-2011, Afghanistan was at its most volatile. The Taliban was more active and more determined than ever to kill as many U.S. Marines as possible. The change in lifestyle is more pronounced for those of us who have experienced direct combat abroad. It is a requirement upon returning to civilian life that we must try to reprogram ourselves, rearranging our psyche in order to fit back into society, trading the mindset of Marine for that of a civilian. This overhaul of personality, when coupled with traumatic experiences in war can midwife temptations to self-medicate and self-destruct. Positive outlets for frustration and combat stress can be difficult to identify and refine but provide one with a far more therapeutic way of coping with the difficulties unique to combat veterans. Justin has successfully located his querencia, and within that space he is able to craft poetry and short stories that help him come to terms with what he saw in Afghanistan and the difficulties of coming home. His poetry is both poignant and realistic in its discussion of subjects that are oftentimes difficult to address. Feelings of doubt, guilt and suicide can become overwhelming when veterans reflect on their combat experiences, but Justin takes these issues head-on, allowing readers candid access into his deepest emotions. The purpose of this book is not to glorify war, or to make any political statement regarding U.S. foreign policy, but to address the psychological costs associated with IED detection, direct combat, returning home, and finding constructive ways to address PTSD. I sincerely hope that as many veterans as possible read Justin's book and gain something positive from what he has written because it is demonstrative of the reality that all of us are susceptible to the psychological strain that accompanies combat. Justin shows how being able to speak unreservedly of this reality is a sign of strength and self-improvement, demonstrating the best qualities of America's veterans.

Andrew Lutz
April 6, 2018 Washington, D.C.

PREFACE

When I was a young child, I would help my mother around our house with chores, yardwork, and laundry. She was at that time a single mother, raising me alone, as she did for the majority of my childhood. I would see my father on select days and weekends of the month, but most of my time growing up was spent with her.

She would hand me an allowance once a week, not much—maybe a couple of dollars—but it sufficed. I worked for weeks and weeks to save up enough money so I could buy a certain music album. Now, looking back, I realize that the album I wanted wasn't what most kids would want to listen to, and my mom was in shock I wanted it as well. I wanted to purchase All Eyez on Me, double disc edition, by Tupac Shakur. I always saw him on the TV on talk shows, and in the news, heard his music on the radio, and ultimately came to the conclusion that he was a very ingenious person. There were times when the only thing on every news channel was Tupac, and at my mom's house we watched the news every night at dinner. I was consumed; there was something I admired in him, and I looked to him as a role model.

Now, I understand as most people read this they're probably judging how my mother raised me and wondering why a child would look up to someone who most people associate with "negative demeanor."

Most people don't know the true Tupac Shakur; most people don't see him for what he was; most saw only how the media portrayed him.

My mother has always shown me it's best to be myself. She always taught me to think for myself—not to judge a book by its cover—and most importantly, that goals are always attainable through hard work and persistence. Believing in myself was a huge aspect of being raised by her. She showed me that by believing in myself I could do anything that my mind could construct.

I saw those same qualities in Tupac. Even as a child, I saw this and noticed it. I felt there was a connection from him to me, and if you're a fan of Pac, I'm positive you can relate. From the time I bought that album, I changed profoundly. So many lessons are to be learned in his music—life lessons that are true to this day, and will hold true until the end of time. I was just scratching the surface.

Then one day, when I was seven years old, he passed away.

I understand most people reading this are skeptical of the abilities of my memory bank at seven years old and wonder how I could remember such a time, but it was such a profound time in my life. Years went on, and Tupac's mother kept releasing his music to the fans. He had an abundant amount of music he recorded before his demise. He knew his time on Earth wasn't going to be long, but just long enough to change the world. He prophesized his own death and could foresee the coming events.

The man had a cloud he could never avoid, and he knew this. In late 1999, Tupac's estate released his poetry book, titled *A Rose That Grew from Concrete*. It was a collection of poetry that Tupac had written from 1989 to 1991. I was a little older by then, and with birthday money I went to the bookstore and purchased it myself. It was enthralling and creative. I had never read poetry seriously, but I loved this so much.

I mimicked Tupac in that regard as time went on, and I started to write poetry on anything from the heartache of being an only child with my mother, to the constant changing of schools because I didn't get along with classmates or teachers. Nothing ever stayed the same. I went to three elementary schools, one middle school, and two different high schools. Poetry helped me with the constant change and inconsistent life that I was living. The single mother working nonstop to raise her son, the uneasy relationships I had with educational institutions, and the relationship with my father while growing up. The one person who truly understood who I was and didn't look at me as some annoying, obnoxious kid was my mother. She embraced my love for Tupac and embraced me as this kid who was never really one to run with the crowd. The majority of the time, I just did my own thing. I never had a core set of friends while growing up. I was always at new schools, so starting and creating a bond with people was hard.

In high school, when I finally settled in to the school I would graduate from, I had embedded myself with a great group of friends, and I felt as if I finally belonged to a crew. I will always be thankful for those people letting me in even though I had not grown up with them since childhood, like the rest. Poetry sort of took the backseat while I was in high school, but Tupac's music was always on cue and was always being played. As I got older, I never forgot or abandoned my admiration for Tupac. He was and still is at the forefront of my mind as one of the main influences of my entire life. He still is to this day.

After losing close family members and a best friend to death and being out of school for almost a year, I realized I needed to make some moves and make a decision for my life. I decided one day with my cousin Robert to enlist into the United States Marine Corps. I had no thoughts of poetry or illusions of a lifestyle of grandeur. I just needed to do something I was going to love, and the USMC was in my opinion the best place for me to go. Running around in the woods with a rifle and compass. Going to the rifle ranges, wearing a military uniform, and the feeling of truly belonging to something greater than myself. It was a dream.

That dream quickly turned into a nightmare over the course of 2010 and 2011. Our deployments overseas were not walking around a distant base, going to some KFC, and taking showers every night. Our deployments were living outside the wire, running out of food sometimes, no showers for months, and direct combat on a weekly basis. All this while trying to mitigate the IED threat that was plaguing Afghanistan. Life seemed to be of little value while we were deployed overseas, and everywhere we went, chaos followed. We pushed into the most dangerous areas of operations in southern Afghanistan during my two deployments. Our battalion took a huge hit over the years I was there. More pain and suffering would consume everyone who went over there and served in those austere environments under harsh conditions. Poetry and Tupac weren't on my mind, and the only thing I was ever thinking about was IEDs and staying alive throughout my time there.

As I came home and began to shift back into the civilian world, I started to really suppress a ton of my memories and emotions from overseas. I would talk to people about certain non-traumatic events that happened in OEF, the ones I could speak about without getting consumed by the chaos. I never spoke about my roommate who passed away, or the guys I saw flying in the air, half torn apart. These memories were locked in a box buried underneath my most challenging memories. I left them there and lived like that for many years.

There was one book I always kept next to

my bed, and I would read it casually every now and again. That was *A Rose That Grew from Concrete*. It was something that helped me out, I think, in the aftermath of serving in combat. The poems started to speak to me in a new way I had never envisioned before. They held real depth that I could truly find connections to. I would try to read a poem a day, and once I had finished the book, I would start over two-thirds of the way in, and so on and so forth. Tupac's poetry was pulling someone out inside me whom I had buried and tried my hardest to forget about. He was speaking to my damaged soul in a way I never had thought possible. I found a new outlet for my pent-up aggression and volatile thinking.

Poetry. I would start back up writing poetry, but this time the poetry would be nothing but combat poetry, nothing but the chaotic, haunting combat that we as a generation experienced in OEF. I wanted to transfer this onto paper, and I wanted to show the world what we went through in southern Afghanistan during the height of OEF. I wanted to bring the reader to a place to which no one had brought a reader before: on the ground in combat with a metal detector, scanning for non-metallic IEDs. I wanted people to experience what we experienced.

I've never been so sure of something in my entire life. This was my calling: to write combat poetry and give it to the world, and hopefully the world would see it, read it, and go through it like I went through it.

I figured that if I was myself, and I put my heart and soul into my poetry, people would see it for what it is and embrace it. To my surprise, everyone did with my first volume of combat poetry and short stories. I've been beyond elated to share my poetry with the world and share it with everyone from every facet of life. So many positive things have happened since the release of my first book. I've met so many people along the way on this journey, so many doors have opened, and most of all, I have a son being born.

My life has changed for the better, and I am no longer suppressing my thoughts, memories, or the events that took place overseas. I am transparent these days, and it truly stems from having the ability to be myself at a young age and knowing exactly what I want and how I want to do it. If you are yourself, people will appreciate that, and people will see that in you. It will pay itself back to you. Tupac Shakur showed me this as a young boy, and my mom encouraged me to act on it and never doubt myself and my abilities. So here I am, dropping my second poetry book for the world to see and feel.

I truly hope everyone enjoys it.

Jack of All Trades - Ben Cantwell

TABLE OF CONTENTS

Headed Back

Walking past the motor pool
The air smells of burn pit and diesel fuel.
Clearing our rifles as we're entering the chow hall,
Walking around base seeing contractors wearing
shawls.
Thirty-minute time limit on the computers.
The MWRs line is full of shooters.
This is the good life
Full of laundry and showers,
But the worst part is we'll be leaving in a few hours.
Got more ammo,
More chow and tons of water.
Headed back to the fight
Outside The Wire.

Full of Tradition

As I hold my A2 with minimal practice,
The drill instructor screams, "You fucking maggots!!"
Go-fasters and glow belts just out of receiving,
Straight up boots, naïve and willing.
We move faster and faster, being pushed to our limits.
Then we pushed past that with a sharp left pivot.
Initial drill and field day all for fun,
Heading into the woods, following compass under moon
and sun.
The United States Marine Corps is full of tradition
From 1775 to post-9/11.

Fighting Rarely Stops

Immersed in Afghanistan,
Our eyes trained on the ground in this land.
Fighting rarely stops—
Seemingly fighting the boogeyman.

Orders

Orders to go left,
Suggestions to go right,
No matter the direction
We're bound for a fight.

The Unknown

The unknown pushes most away
When the unknown should invite most to stay.

Night, Night

Night-night
Says the bomb dropped from flight.

Ground troops in contact,
Engaged with an enemy that's out of sight.

First Light

Unstrapping my Kevlar and dropping my flak,
Untying my boots and stretching my back.
The sun is down as we roll back inside the wire,
Covered in moon dust, all of us dead tired.
Break out the cots and hook up the hammocks,
Our platoon works in unison as a perfect dynamic.
Squad leaders control the fire team leaders.
Three tents over are the Marine Raiders.
It's time to unwind and relax for the night
Because we roll out tomorrow at first light.

Firefight

The sun moves through the trees.
IEDs bring Marines to their knees.
240s hip-fired on the move,
Lobbing 40 mike mike,
Getting in the groove.
Fire power is shrouded by Death,
Rounds impacting with each step.

Skirmishes

Skirmishes at dawn...
IEDs oblige hands-on.
Back home, you're withdrawn.

IEDS

It's loud.
The pressure is paralyzing.
My flak compresses my spine;
The pressure squeezes my mind.
Noise turns to silence as my ears mute the racket.
Nothing can prepare you—
No form of practice.

Beyond Death

IEDs hidden,
Never knowing your last step—
Life is beyond death.

One in the Chamber

The frustrations of my haunted make their way in.
At the same time inserted was the firing pin.
They move like ghosts, mocking my pain,
But within my skull these demons are contained.
One in the chamber
And it shall remain
Until the day it's needed to destroy my brain!

P for Plenty

Day to day
The violence trapped in my brain—
Everywhere I go I seem to myself a bane,
Craving the violence I once was embedded,
Patrolling the streets while carrying my weapon.
It's lasting memories that keep me up and awake
throughout the night.
Dreams, not nightmares, keep me yearning for the fight.
The warrior mentality controls my conscious,
Practice after practice
Makes operations flawless.
Empty magazines in a full dump pouch,
"P" for plenty when in doubt.

Alpha

Automatics aim across abandoned architecture,
aiding an Afghan army, assuring an attack against
amateur aggressors.

Reloading

The sky speaks through the stars,
Enemies want to play, so we earn our CARs.
Night as bright as the day,
All we see is green,
Tracers impacting over the ravine.
"Reloading!" shouts a Marine.

Indicators

My demons still sweeping, scanning and
Analyzing everything inside every moment.
Waiting and anticipating that reflection mirroring off
that copper wire,
The difference in the half-wet ground next to the dry,
or the smallest piece Of plastic sticking through the
gravel.
Everywhere they go you find them,
The IEDs were everything,
So they consumed everyone in every place.

You're All Alone

Dark thoughts,
Deep depression
In Afghanistan,
Daily stressin'.
Marines are lost,
Buried at home.
When you come back
You're all alone.
Take me to that time in the road
When our truck got hit
As we felt it explode
From underneath
The ground it grew,
Changing our lives—
If we only knew.
TBI from the piercing percussion.
No medevac today—
We stay for the mission.

Conflict

All of us enrolled.
Conflict resides in our soul
Still out on patrol.

Dazed and Confused

You can hear the whistle
Moments before impact.
It doesn't take long
To realize you're under attack.
Like a firework
Going off in my face,
A loud, paralyzing boom,
Shrapnel all over the place.
Blown off my feet by blast,
Dazed and confused,
The shrapnel still flying past.
Ringing fills my head instantly.
The memory will always last.

Contact Left

Troops in contact—
Contact left!
Point and shoot
In dispute.
The enemy moves
Quick and quiet.
We fight rough
While they're non-compliant.

Steady

Stretchers on trucks—
We'll use them when ready.
Blasts going off
While my trigger finger is steady.

The Earth Seas

The earth breathes,
The earth seas,
Encompassing us all,
For we will never leave,
Keeping us attached
At our feet,
Forever resisting the pull
With each step.

Repeat

Eternally bound to the Afghan streets,
Sweep and dig, then gunfight/repeat.

Promise, Hope, Fear and Denial

Last week was filled with promise and hope, but hope
was medevac'd from
a shot to the throat.
Promise took a blast right outside camp, he's still
alive, only now a triple
amp.

They've been replaced by Fear and Denial, each one
carrying a brand new
rifle.
Combat intimidates the new and the old, every day
new routes are being
patrolled.
Fear was scared in his first battle, luckily was backed
up by a guy named
Denial.

Molotov

Overthinking is a gift and a curse that kept me alive overseas but hinders me now when I'm back on the streets.
Everything is a trap waiting to go off, or am I overthinking, expecting the Molotov?
My thoughts are consumed with over-analyzing, over-calculating, and IEDs hidden; but now that I'm home, my thoughts become the villain.

Constrained

"Hand me the blasting caps!"
He shouts as rounds impact,
Prepping the C4 during the attack.
They ambushed our POS
C.O.C. sees them coming with GBOSS.
Rocket teams with RPGs—
Over thirty of them coming across.
It's a weekly event that always ends in loss.
They bait us in with IEDs,
Knowing we'll eliminate them with ease,
So they send in their rocket teams
And train their anti-aircraft gun at me.
I'm not a plane; I'm a Marine
Walking on patrol, finding IEDs,
Carrying my flak riddled with ammo
Sweat and sand covering my fatigues.
Together we form a fierce fighting force
Designed to fight just as mean or worse.
Rounds snap, and magazines are drained
ROEs have you feeling constrained.

Misfits

Misfits of Marjah,
High-priced gear we're in charge of.
Headed from Garmsir.

Bravo

Bandages block blood, batteries below brown boots,
bold bomb builder breeds brilliance, battle breaks
balancing brains.

Never Become Accustomed

Unknown under the ground,
Unknown around the corner,
Unknown is everywhere in this land of horror.
The only thing that's known is death
and loss of limbs.
No matter how many times,
It'll always make you cringe.
You never become accustomed to losing your friends.

Follow Me

Follow me.
Follow in my steps
As our boots hit the ground,
Always alert,
Metal detectors making a sound.
We're being watched
While we patrol this valley.
Eyes everywhere,
Hiding in the alley.
RPG teams enclose our position
But are swiftly eradicated by a fire mission.

Sangin Valley

Sangin Valley, 2011
Into it we breached, the opposite of heaven.

Gone is the Love

Withdrawn from reality,
Each minute magazines are emptied,
Anxiously stepping and sweeping.
Each hour this process is repeating.
My mind escapes when back in the wire
To a place that's quiet and free of indirect fire.
Our realities are harsh, but we adapt and love it that
way—
Minimalist living out here day to day
Never far do we let our minds stray.
Gone is the love
Replaced by the hate,
Each week seeing your boys disintegrate,
Enemy movements at night keeping us awake.

Thoughts of Violence

Thoughts of violence fill my mind,
Every single day creeping up my spine.
The thoughts persist, actively plotting
To destroy my world
And those around me.

Missing

Something is missing—
Something I hate; at the same time crave—
Something like death
Holding its scythe beside an early grave.

Aggressive

Warriors stretched out thin,
Fighting endlessly each chance,
Aggressive in stance.

GWOT TrapLordz OEF

31 North and 63 East—
This is where you'll find our clarity increased.
Helmand Valley Gun Club is a brotherhood of warriors,
from Now-Zad, Marjah, and Sangin our
battlefields are notorious.
Close the feed tray cover and rack it back twice.
Adjust the T&E whilst aiming down the sights.
Murkin in Marjah or Bangin in Sangin,
Every single step we're sweeping and clearing.
BIPing IEDs while shooting tow missiles
When IDF comes, you'll hear the whistle.
HIMARS all day flying high in the sky,
While everyone is watching, we're taking
shit from supply.

We're the GWOT TRAPLORDZ;
Pop smoke on that wall charge—
We're not taking the door.

GWOT TrapLordz OIF

32 North and 41 East-
This is where you'll find our clarity increased.
Anbar province Gun Club is a brotherhood of warriors,
from Baghdad, Fallujah and Ramadi our
battlefields are notorious.
Close the feed tray cover and rack it back twice.
Adjust the T&E whilst aiming down the sights.
Mobbin in Mosul or fighting in Fallujah
Every single house we're stackin' and clearin'
Throwing frags in rooms and shooting tow missiles
When IDF comes, you'll hear the whistle.
Warthogs all day flying high in the sky,
While everyone is watching, we're taking
shit from supply.

We're the GWOT TRAPLORDZ;
Knock knock motherfucker-
We're kicking in the door.

No, You're Home

Coming home, war rages on.
In my mind, ammo is worn
For tonight we fight!
No, you're home.
Seek peace in your mind.
Release the magazine and reload.
Stop this nonsense, for you are home.
Everyday battles take place within my dome.
We fight ourselves upon returning home.

Into Hell

Degenerates and misfits
Enlisted for themselves but realize over time they
enlisted into hell.
Half-torn-apart bodies lying in craters
While men scream for their mothers, these hard
operators.
Gunshots come in while the medevac goes out.
How many men leave us—you'll be scared by the
amount.
Day after day we keep fighting and pushing,
Our eyes on the ground, steadily looking.

If I Fail

If I fail, tell my family I did my best.
I'm coming home on my final trip, being laid to rest.
If I fail, I didn't pass my would-be-final test,
But if I failed, I finished my ultimate quest.
I long for this life or I wouldn't have come,
Don't be sad, Mom and Dad, my pain is finally numb.

Charlie

C4 combusts, creating certain chemical claps, close
compounds containing cowardly combatants

Stalking in the Night

The population goes into hiding when we start stalking
in the night.
Condition one as the sun goes down, ready for the fight.
We push back on the enemy that's keeping us here.
Silently moving with the night, using hand signals, we
disappear.

Mariah's Hair

Occupied is my mind.
I find myself scanning the ground
Looking for something,
Finding discrepancies and differences in color, shape,
and texture,
My mind convinced,
Pupils going left, going right, up and down,
Traversing over the earth in front of me.
I realize I'm looking for something that's not even there.

I take a step back and look to see the wind drifting
through Mariah's hair.
My mind is still overseas at times. It makes my eyes
unable to see
The beauty that lies directly in front of me.

Phantom

Phantom muzzle flash—
Movements while firing hot brass.
Never use same path.

No Politics

Triggers are pulled on the exhale,
The bolt ejecting the brass.
"They're right out in front!"
Shouts the Marine in the grass.
Rounds impacting all around,
Fiercely snapping past.
The fight just got real—
Marines digging into position.
We've prepared for this.
We're incredibly efficient—
240s and 40 mike mike
SAWs and 5.56.
Down here in the dirt there are no politics.

Beloved by All

Today is like tomorrow.
For today we celebrate.
We praise the insane,
The few who have no restraint,
The ones who remained
After all was erased.
The IED goes off
While sealing our fate,
Removing us altogether from this space.
We become memories
And names on a wall
Beloved by all
And missed most of all.

Contact Front

Through poppy fields we patrol.
Fighting the enemy,
We're always in control.
With superior firepower we advance.
Aggressive and on point is our stance.
Recon's overwatch always take the shot, given the
chance.
Our boots are soaked from irrigation,
Sniper teams up top for observation.
Attitudes of the men promote hate and lament,
Jumping over ditches with a 240 is a dreaded event.
"Contact Front!"
The sweeper screams
As he drops behind cover to his knees.
Adrenaline flows as rounds snap past,
We must be harder, faster and smarter
If we are to last.

Everyday Life

Long patrols sweeping in and out the wadi,
Our feelings come and go but are always shoddy.
We can never be sure where is the hiding hadji.
We fight and take cover throughout our days.
Nonstop confrontation is the only thing that stays.
Complacency covers some people's mind like a glaze.
I promise this is everyday life,
Not just a phase.

Shellshocked

We try to move fast.
Arduous combat is vast.
Shell-shocked from the blast.

Ghosts

Ghosts in the valley
Patrolling in the alleys:
Warfare finale

Teamwork

Working as a team,
Communicating out loud,
Explosives are found.

Nightfall

Nightfall goons come out.
Moving in silence we prowl...
NODs drop on my scowl.

Shadows

Shadows become foes,
Reaching out with bombs in roads,
Waiting for patrols.

Green Eyes

Enemies emplace,
Sun sets, green eyes on my face.
Fighting, we embrace.

Delta

Det-cord detonates, destroying discoverable
devices deliberately disguised, damaging deployed
disciplined defenders.

Hellbelt

Hellbelt 203
Lobbing 'nades at enemies,
Vicious tendencies.

Moonrise

Sunset, then moonrise.
Frog gear, torn seams at my thighs.
NODs cover my eyes.

Goon Squad

Goon Squad preps with haste,
Ready to seal someone's fate.
Terp goes to translate.

Expedient Bangalores

Engineer stakes filled with C4—
Double it up for an expedient Bangalore.
Breaching defenses with a bang,
Marines move in on the flank.

Legacy

Mission briefings every morning:
LT lays the groundwork for the tactical warning.
We're ready to go fight our enemy.
Loading magazines, we're leaving a legacy.

The Night

The night shows stars you'll never see again
Stretched out across the sky,
The darkness trying to fit in.
A billion lights peppered in the night,
Condition one, preparing for the fight
Like little lights illuminating the sky.
Glowing radiant, the light intensifies,
Rounding each corner,
NVGs over eyes.

Apparitions

Adversaries move
Like apparitions, immune
To chaos and doom.

Nowhere To Go

Darkness fills the sky above us as we
take cover from the IDF—
Nowhere to go,
Nowhere to hide,
Nothing to save you from the debris.
Shrapnel flies past my face; the pressure
sweeps me off my feet.
The deafening sound pierces my heartbeat.
Earsplitting is the sound, and it's known instantly.
The whistle of the incoming rounds
prepares you rapidly,
Ripping apart all in the vicinity
nothing stands a chance.
Never once did I think I would find myself
in this circumstance.

Dreams

Sunsets here are things of dreams, perpetuating love
all over, it would seem.

Instead, the atmosphere is filled with hate. Darkness
eternally seals our fate.

Flawless

Failing is not a choice.
Pull out your demons, then face them in the arena
of your conscious.
Push them out, forcing the confrontation,
and keeping your promise.
Fight them to the end,
Never giving in,
Never giving up, finding solace.
Win the battles in your mind. Then you will be flawless.

Spewing Hate

The barrel breathes fierce fire,
Spewing hate at the cyclic rate,
Never giving the enemy enough time to acclimate.

Watchful Eye

Combat dropping into a foreign land.
This place has been fighting since before I was born.
Afghanistan knows no laws, it is destined to be scorned.
Through poppy fields we patrol, mixed with the corn.
The enemy keeps a watchful eye on passing troops,
and they learn.

Echo

Explosive experiences enduring eternally expose
extraordinary encounters exceeding expectations.

Light Or Dark

Understanding my mind is a task
Designed for only those who can last.
Your eyes cannot see what we have seen, but you can
try to see into our dreams.
Light or dark, we will never let you down.
If you reach out for clarity, we will not let you drown.
Pulling you into our thoughts and our minds,
Opening you up to our space and our time.

Eyes Cannot See

The eyes cannot see the pain trapped in my brain,
The same brain and eyes where these memories
were obtained.

The Acceptable Norm

Our war is background noise.
Society pushes on, accepting something is going on,
But never fully understanding that we've all
come and gone.
Our forgotten war or the acceptable norm?
We've been in combat for half the time since I was born.
In 2001 when our towers were torn, they were
taken from us and we have steadily mourned.
Warriors come home, and no one bats an eye,
but we have lost our friends
who now live in the sky.
Everyone doesn't acknowledge the fact that men
sacrificed. It seems almost as if nothing
we do will suffice.
People live on with their daily life, never wanting to
see the truth beyond their mind: that young men and
women have paid the ultimate price.

Plant A Seed

They plant a seed
Where we take a knee,
Triggering a tree
That destroys all we see.
That tree is death,
And death comes swift
From the loud blast
You feel your life shift.

Glory

Battle cry in the form of overwhelming firepower,
We push into hell without any cover fire.
Ducking and weaving to avoid the rounds,
Marines finally take cover behind the compound.
Bounding across open fields, we push
into unknown territory,
Never knowing our last step, it doesn't matter...
for here we find our glory.

Uncover and Discover

Rack one back.
Thumb takes it off safety.
Glass through your ACOG
Magnifies intensely.
Spider holes they fire
As we take cover.
IED after IED
We uncover and discover.

Reminders

The headstones above the graves remind us of a road
that's been paved
Generations before, and the blood that they gave.

The Full Moon

The full moon shines bright on the Marines.
With NVGs they're low-crawling to the ravine,
Setting up an over-watch position to catch the
enemy, who is always emplacing.
Find the one who digs in the ground before the main
element comes through with the mine hounds.
No one knows who the bomb maker is; they just know
he's great with his wits,
Creating bombs and traps that have no metal,
Wounding and killing Marines—
that's the opposite of gentle.
The power source is strung into the field,
...Or is underneath the explosive highly concealed.

Wraiths

Hellish wraiths fighting,
IEDs burst like lightning,
Patrols frightening.

Foxtrot

Fresh firefights forever freezing frame for frame from foreign fields feature fierce fighting favoring fearless friends.

Trailblazer Two

It's been seven days since we arrived at Camp Leatherneck, and finally we're about to head out on our first mission that isn't a rip mission. We're finally going to head out beyond the wire, as a platoon. We've been training months for this. For some of us, this is our second deployment, but for many it is their first. As for me and most of the NCOs, it is our second time in a route clearance team headed to mitigate the IED threat that is consuming southern Afghanistan.

Route clearance teams have a certain order in which they operate. We have two Huskies up front, scanning with metal detection and ground-penetrating radar, a lead gun truck to navigate the Huskies, and the platoon, to provide security and to get out of the truck and conduct foot patrol sweeps. A second gun truck does the same work as the first, minus the navigation. The Buffalo comes after that.

The Buffalo's job was to come up and interrogate any possible IEDs that couldn't be handled by the two gun truck sweep teams. Behind the Buffalo we had two gun trucks for security, a wrecker driven by our mechanic SGT Naylor, a seven-ton loaded with the his gear and any possible items we would need as a platoon, and finally a rear gun truck providing rear security.

As bad as it may sound, the Husky is designed to be torn apart by IEDs. The operators of these Huskies drive slowly and pay attention to their monitors and sounds while scanning. My job was lead gun truck vehicle commander/navigator, so my truck was the first gun truck behind the Huskies. If they missed an IED, we were going to get hit, or another truck behind us would be.

Navigating the Huskies through Afghanistan was one of many responsibilities I had as lead gun truck commander. On this particular mission, my decision-making abilities would come into play, but I was yet to realize this.

The mission seemed simple enough: We would spearhead a convoy of U.S. Navy Seabees up to a FOB in Now-Zad, which was in the middle of a valley at the base of the mountain ranges north of Camp Leatherneck. Our job was to ensure the Seabees arrived safely so they could de-mil the FOB.

Simple enough, I thought. I'll find a good route that hasn't been traversed before on my BFT, and I'll navigate this entire convoy to their destination. Having been a machine gunner on my first deployment to Marjah, and being close friends with the platoon's previous guide (Sgt. Matisi), I felt ready. Matisi had shown me and trained me for this particular job and actually requested that I take up the mantle for this next deployment.

Navigating the entire platoon all over southern Afghanistan had its challenges. There was one paved road, which stretched east to west, called Route One. It was a two-lane highway, which was used as a main supply route, but our area of operations wasn't on Route One; it was north of it.

We pushed outside the wire of Camp Leatherneck, my gun truck out front. We didn't need to utilize the Huskies until we were off the main route and into territory that had no over-watch. While were pushing east down Route One, all the trucks followed, the Navy Seabees behind our rear gun truck, relying on us to get them to their final destination safely. I was on the BFT, scanning, and trying to find the best route to take once off Route One and heading north to Now-Zad. I found a solid path to take that seemed to be the best route.

Once off the road and far enough away from Route One, we halted the convoy and pushed the Huskies out front to start scanning. This is where we slowed down and let the Husky operators do their jobs. Each moment was a million moments because this was our first mission as a whole, and our first mission outside the wire on this deployment, so we were all on edge.

The platoon we replaced looked like they'd been through hell and back, and they were happy to finally be leaving. We were happy to finally be back. Most of us weren't at the bottom of the barrel on this deployment, so we were eager to show the higher-ups that we were highly capable individuals, who were good enough to run a platoon ourselves as NCOs.

Route Clearance Team Two, call-sign Trailblazer Two, had a platoon commander, Lt. Brooks, a platoon sergeant, Gunnery Sergeant Wodrich, and zero sergeants. Several of us were E-4s, and we needed to prove that we were ready for this trial by fire.

There was no leadership on the engineer side except for the platoon commander and platoon sergeant. No sergeants or staff sergeants were in between the corporals and Gunny, so we needed to be in top form. The only sergeant we had in the platoon was Sgt. Naylor, our mechanic, and he didn't get involved in engineer politics. Our first mission needed to be a success. My truck and the NCOs in the platoon were determined to be the best route clearance engineers that our company had.

The day seemed to be dragging on and on. These Huskies were scanning, and we weren't getting anything back. Radio chatter was low; the only one talking on COMM was myself, to the Huskies, directing them on the route that had already been pre-planned on my BFT coming up here. At each compound we passed, the gunners were on high alert. In my truck, we had PFC Cotton, who was a great gunner and could reload a .50 faster than most people. That's why he was the lead gun truck gunner.

He kept a watchful eye as we crept past

compounds and was always looking out for IEDs that the Huskies might have missed. My eyes were shifting from the BFT and back to the Huskies, making adjustments over COMM when needed.

My lieutenant came over the radio: "Drago to Faded Line." His call sign was "Drago," like Dolph Lundgren's character in the Rocky films. He was his doppelganger: LT. Brooks was tall, blond, and built like a house. He had played college football, and you could tell. My personal call sign, along with my truck's call sign, was "Faded Line," as in sweeping for IEDs you're walking the faded line between life and death.

"Send it, Drago," I responded.

"The Seabees have a tire blowout midway in their convoy."

"Roger. ALL HALT, ALL HALT," I echoed on the radio for our platoon to stop moving.

"They need security while they change it. Have your truck swing back around with a Husky and provide security for them while they change it," the lieutenant said.

"Roger that, sir. We are on our way."

I looked over at LCpl. Brown, the driver of our truck. He could hear everything that was being said, he nodded in agreement. "Let me get Regan to come around, and then we'll head back there," I said to LT.

"Faded Line to Regan."

"Send it," he replied.

"Hey, I need you to wrap around and escort

my truck to the downed Seabees' location."

"Roger," he said as his vehicle turned around and started making its way toward us. It was standard operating procedure to be escorted by a Husky whenever we needed to take a truck to the rear of the convoy or take a lone truck somewhere. The downed Seabee truck was almost near the end of the convoy, which was pretty far from Trailblazer Two. The Seabees had roughly 30 vehicles for this mission, with our platoon included it was long convoy stretched out.

We pulled up to the Navy Seabee truck that had the flat. The sweeper in the back of the truck, Cpl Pressley, and I hopped out with our metal detectors and started sweeping around the Seabees' truck. It took us a little over ten minutes to deem the area clear of any IEDs or mines. Once cleared, the Seabees jumped out and started getting to work on replacing their old tire with the new tire. I stayed outside the truck and started talking to the Seabees.

"How'd you guys manage to flat a tire out here?" I asked with some sarcasm because I knew the terrain was rough and very difficult.

They laughed, acknowledging my sarcasm. "Oh, you know—we ran over a nail," one of them shot back at me with the same sarcasm.

I chuckled a little. "Yeah, I can see that happening, haha," I replied.

Just as I replied, a snap came in. CRACK!

I took cover behind our mine-roller, which was connected to our truck, raised my rifle, and started glassing through the ACOG optic scanning over the barren land in front of me.

"Cotton! Where is it?!" I shouted up to Cotton, who already had binoculars to his eyes and was also scanning the area in front of us.

"I'm looking, I'm looking," he called back down to me.

I turned around to see if the Seabees were grabbing rifles because we were about to be in a gunfight, but to my surprise they were gone. They all had taken cover behind their truck. "Are we getting shot at?!" one of them asked me. I could hear in his voice that this kid was not happy, and the sarcasm he had been spewing out before had turned to petrified terror.

"Yeah, man, we are. We're going to find where it's coming from, then eliminate them," I said with enough confidence to hopefully ease his mind. I shuffled back to the mine-roller and duck-bent over so I was somewhat concealed. SNAP! Another round came in, and this time I could tell by the sound that the round was impacting in front of us. I couldn't see where the fire was coming from being this low behind the mine-roller.

"I got him! He's about 1500 meters away from us. I can see him in the bushes next to the compound far away, looks like he's firing an AK." Cotton tells me from the gunner's turret. Since the enemy combatant was using an AK47 and was 1500 meters out, I knew for a fact he wasn't going to be able to effectively engage us, so I climbed back into the VC seat of the truck leaving the door open. Cotton started letting loose on the .50, effectively engaging the enemy. Within moments the firing was over and the enemy was eliminated.

"He's down!" Cotton said with a winning grin covering his face as we dropped back in the truck.

"Good shit, man! You handled that asshole the only way Marines know how, with overwhelming firepower." I laughed, Cotton started laughing, Brown started laughing, and Pressley started laughing as we all rejoiced in the minor victory our truck had just had. We handled that situation flawlessly according to us: We located the enemy, engaged him, and eliminated him within moments.

I jumped back out of the truck to check on the Navy Seabees.

"Is he dead?" one of them asked, looking up at me.

"Yes. We eliminated the threat so you guys can finish changing your tire," I said and then walked back to my truck and got back in.

I got on the radio and started up COMM with LT. "Faded Line to Drago," I said.

"Send it, Faded line," LT responded.

"We engaged and eliminated one target,

roughly 1500 meters away. He was engaging us and the Seabees but is now mitigated."

"Roger that. I'll send it up," he replied.

Our truck was still smiling thirty minutes after the engagement. We'd been on this mission for a little over four hours and in country for seven days; we'd had our first gunfight, and it had been executed flawlessly. This is what Marines do: We fight, and we love it.

Once the Seabees were finished changing their tire and were ready to go, we followed the Husky back to the front of the convoy. We positioned ourselves exactly where we'd left off and kept pushing. More arduous terrain and more slow, drawn-out driving. The life of a route clearance team was like this—very high and intense activity, followed by slow, tedious movements. We pushed on for another couple of hours with no sort of excitement, just the casual radio chatter directing and navigating the Huskies, and everyone else driving in the path I put us on.

It was getting later in the day, near the afternoon, when the route we were on could no longer be driven. The route came to an end at a steep wadi, and the only way to go was left or right. Just past the wadi was a good-sized hill, and where we needed to be was a few klicks beyond that hill.

I could see the FOB on the BFT, and the only way around this hill was to make the decision to go left or to go right. If we went left, there were cornfields, and we would be driving along the edge of the wadi. If one of the trucks got hit by an IED, it would roll over and into the wadi, which wouldn't be good at all. If we went right, that seemed to be the easier option since it was less steep, and we could get on the other side of the wadi and push pretty smoothly next to the large hill to go around it.

If we went right, though, there were two compounds with about 50 meters between them, and there looked to be no one living in them, which could mean the enemy was using them as cover and concealment.

"Faded Line to Drago."

"Send it," LT said.

"Sir, we have a situation. We cannot continue going straight. We need to either go left or go right to get through this wadi, then move around that hill to get to the FOB," I relayed to LT.

"Okay, Eggen. Make your best judgment," he responded. Much to my surprise, he was giving me this task and trusting I'd make the right decision here.

"Roger that, sir. I'm going to take the two Huskies to the right and see if we can find a clear path to the opposite side of the wadi," I told him over the radio. "Faded Line to Regan."

"Go for Regan," he said.

"Let's go right and try to find a suitable path to take this convoy through that wadi," I said.

"Good to go," he replied as he started driving closer to the wadi and searching for a path that wasn't as steep and was not going to be dangerous for the Navy Seabee trucks to pass through.

After moments of him and the second Husky riding along the bank, they found a smooth spot to drive through. "Regan to Faded Line."

"Go for Faded Line," I said.

"I found a path that's going to be easy enough for the rest of the convoy to make it through and smooth enough to get to the other side of the wadi," he relayed to me over COMM.

"Good to go. Have Bulldog follow you through once you've cleared it and on the other side." (Bulldog was the call sign for the second Husky, a tough SOB named Cpl. McEwan.)

"Roger that," Regan said, followed by, "Roger that," from McEwan.

Regan in his Husky started going into the wadi, while Bulldog waited his turn. Our gun truck was positioned behind them, scanning for any sort of ambush or attack that could be coming.

Regan cleared the way and was now on the other side of the wadi, roughly 25-35 meters away from one of the compounds. Bulldog started making his way down and into the wadi, but within a couple of seconds of his going in, BOOM!! A loud boom engulfed the area while dust filled our vision and shook us up.

Chunks of metal, tires, and dirt filled the air around us. Bulldog had just got hit. Regan must have just missed the IED, and when Bulldog went in, he rolled over it, or it could've been a pull-string detonation from one of the compounds.

"Faded Line to Bulldog. You okay?"

"Roger, I'm good."

Just as he responded, our truck started taking contact. CLANK! TING! SNAP! The rounds started hitting the side of our truck. "Cotton, get on that shit!" I shouted at Cotton.

"Already on it!" he shouted back to me. The .50 was erupting from the turret. Rounds started impacting on the compounds across the wadi. Regan was alone on the other side. We were taking fire from both compounds, muzzle flashes coming from spider holes in each compound. I realized instantly that they'd chosen to position themselves in this exact location knowing that this was the easiest and most traversable route to get across the wadi. They'd used the IED to isolate the Husky and ambush our truck.

What seemed like an eternity was a matter of moments, and the firing from the compounds stopped once the .50 had opened up and let loose. Cotton reloaded the .50. "Reloading!" he shouted and quickly racked it back twice to start firing off again. A few more seconds went by, and Cotton stopped firing. Nothing was happening, and all was silent.

"Faded Line to Regan."

"Send it, Faded Line."

"Hey, man, push back and start clearing around the other Husky. We need to get Bulldog out of that thing and back to Doc," I said.

"Good to go," he replied and instantly started the process of clearing backward and making his way to our side of the wadi, where the Husky had been blown apart. Regan scanned over the area around the downed Husky and parked it. "Pressley, let's get out and sweep to Bulldog and get him ready for Doc, and let's clear it for Sgt. Naylor and the wrecker."

"Drago to Faded Line," LT radioed in.

"Send it, sir."

"I'm sending the second gun truck to escort the wrecker up there with the seven-ton, so we can get that Husky out of there so we can push on."

"Roger that, sir."

Pressley and I waited until the wrecker and seven-ton were close enough to the downed Husky, just in case one of them hit an IED. We didn't want to be out on the ground if they did. The wrecker and seven-ton showed up, and Pressley and I started sweeping over to the Husky and wrecker, followed by Cpl. Angel, who was the second gun truck VC, sweeping the area. The second gun truck was there for security and escorted the wrecker and seven-ton.

Once everything was deemed clear, the Marines in the wrecker and seven-ton dismounted starting the recovery process of the downed Husky. McEwan was escorted to the second gun truck for the time being, while we recovered his Husky. Sgt. Naylor and LCpl. Phillips were instrumental in the recovery process and were very good at doing their jobs.

"Well, one hit down, who knows how many more to come, this wasn't a good spot, and we need to get out of here" I said to Sgt. Naylor.

"Yup. We just gotta get this Husky up and out of here before we start taking contact again. Being out in the open like this is no good," he replied. Sgt. Naylor kept working on getting the Husky up and on the back of the seven-ton. The rest of us went around and picked up the pieces of the Husky that were strung all over the place, steadily sweeping while doing it.

Once the Husky was loaded and strapped down to the back of the seven-ton, we all went back to our gun trucks to push on and finish the mission. I jumped back into the VC seat of Faded Line, and LT radioed me: "Drago to Faded Line."

"Go for Faded Line."

"I'll write up an after-action report with you and your truck when we get to the destination and forward it to higher." he said.

"Good to go, sir."

Sitting there afterwards I figured out that this was the enemy's plan all along: to channel us into the easiest route and then blast us, then fire on us. We did lose a truck and were down a Husky, but no one was mortally wounded, just a headache on McEwan's end. I got the message from Angel that Doc had cleared McEwan with a MIST exam, and he was just a little rattled. Like I said before, he's a tough SOB. It wasn't his first blast in life, and it wouldn't be his last.

I directed Regan to head left and along the edge of the wadi next to the cornfield. It wasn't the best route, but we'd already been drawn in once, and the harder route was now the only route I chose to take. All the trucks were back in their regular positions, and we started pushing left and finally came to a drivable route through the wadi.

We cleared it and made sure it was easy enough for the Seabees' trucks to drive in and out of. We pushed past the hill that had forced us to make the decision to go left or right. We had lost a Husky, gotten into two gunfights—and it was our first mission in southern Afghanistan in 2011. We had been in country for seven days, and we had seven more months to go. This mission was a learning experience for all of us, and it brought us closer as a platoon. Mistakes had been made, but that's part of going on missions. You learn. Within an hour or two after Bulldog was hit and we were ambushed, we finally arrived at the FOB we were supposed to bring the Seabees to.

It had been a long day, and we were just getting started. There were many more IEDs to find, many more trucks would get hit, more gunfights were to come, and a few more ambushes were in store for Trailblazer Two. That night we settled inside the wire at the FOB, and we all reflected on the day. We set up cots and hammocks, and then we passed out, ready to take on whatever was to come our way outside the wire, when we left the next day.

Glossary of Terms

40 MM - 40 mm grenade
240 - M240 machine gun
A2 - M16 A2 service rifle
ACOG - advanced combat optical gunsight
B.I.P. – blow in place
BFT - blue force tracker
C.A.R. - combat action ribbon
C.O.C. - combat operations center
COMM - communication
FLAK - flak jacket/body armor
FOB - forward operating base
GBOSS - ground based operational surveillance system
GWOT - global war on terrorism
HIMARS - high mobility artillery rocket system
IDF - indirect fire
I.E.D. – improvised explosive device
KLICKS - kilometers
M203 - single shot 40mm under-barrel grenade launcher
MEDEVAC - medical evacuation
M.W.R. - morale, welfare, and recreation
NCO - non-commissioned officer
N.O.D. - night optic devices
N.V.G. - night vision goggles
POS - position
R.O.E. - rules of engagement
R.P.G. – rocket propelled grenade
S.A.W. - squad automatic weapon
T&E - traverse and elevation
VC – vehicle commander

Acknowledgements

This book would not have happened without the love and support from- Mariah, Mom, Dad, Keith, Trish, Preston (Sleepe12), Dennis (Lil D), Grandpa Hatcher, Robert Hatcher and Family, Johnny Fried & Family, Evan Durham, James Bell & Family, Nate Campbell, Brendan Marzan, Patrick Matisi & Family, Mike Maniglia & Family, Jacob Daily, Christopher Carr and The Stay Violent Family, The Khanal's, Kevin Blair, Matthew Dawson & Family, Andrew Lutz, Brian Jones , Ben Cantwell , The Marines of Route Clearance Platoon 2, The Marines Of 2nd Combat Engineer Battalion, Andre Forrest, Dylan Sheehan & Family, Matt Hudson, Brandon (Speedy), the Palm Beach Post, Emporia State University, American University, NC State, Sandee Gertz, My Editor, the Photographics USA Family, and everyone who has purchased one of my books! I thank you all from the bottom of my heart.

Author, Justin Eggen

About the Author

Justin Thomas Eggen was born on March 28th, 1989 in West Palm Beach, FL. A year and a half into his enlistment with the United States Marine Corps he found himself as a Combat Replacement headed to Marjah, Afghanistan in February 2010.

He was a heavy machine gunner for Route Clearance Platoon 2, where he would operate for the next 4 months. 14 months later he was the Lead Gun Truck Commander/ Platoon Navigator for Route Clearance Platoon 2, this time headed to the Sangin Valley. He would spend the most of 2011 operating out of southern Afghanistan during the height of OEF.

In May 2012 he was Honorably Discharged from the Marine Corps and headed back home to FL. Within the next several years he would begin writing and produce *"Outside The Wire: a U.S. Marine's Collection of Combat Poems & Short Stories Volume I"*.

Since the release of his first book, he has continued to write and has many pieces of literature planned for release. He focuses now on *"Outside The Wire: a U.S. Marine's Collection of Combat Poems & Short Stories Volume I,II, & III"*, *"The Art Of Warrior Poetry"* and his new family. He and his girlfriend are expecting a baby boy in the beginning of July 2018.

Coming Soon

"The Art Of Warrior Poetry"

-By Justin T. Eggen

"Outside The Wire: a U.S. Marine's Collection
of Combat Poems & Short Stories
Volume III"

-By Justin T. Eggen

Cover & Sweeper by:
www.bencantwellart.com
IG: @bencantwell_art

"Untitled" 1st Page Artwork by
Matt Hudson
@hudsonfineart

www.outsidethewirebook.com

FB & IG:
@outsidethewirecollection

Email:
outsidethewirebook@gmail.com

Made in the USA
Monee, IL
17 December 2020